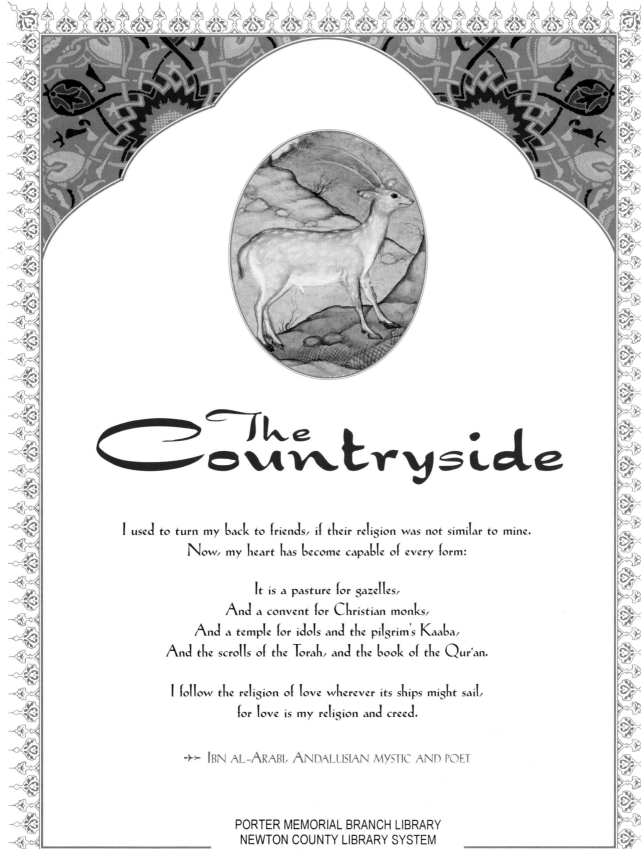

The Countryside

I used to turn my back to friends, if their religion was not similar to mine.
Now, my heart has become capable of every form:

It is a pasture for gazelles,
And a convent for Christian monks,
And a temple for idols and the pilgrim's Kaaba,
And the scrolls of the Torah, and the book of the Qur'an.

I follow the religion of love wherever its ships might sail,
for love is my religion and creed.

➤ IBN AL-ARABI, ANDALUSIAN MYSTIC AND POET

PORTER MEMORIAL BRANCH LIBRARY
NEWTON COUNTY LIBRARY SYSTEM
6191 HIGHWAY 212
COVINGTON, GA 30016

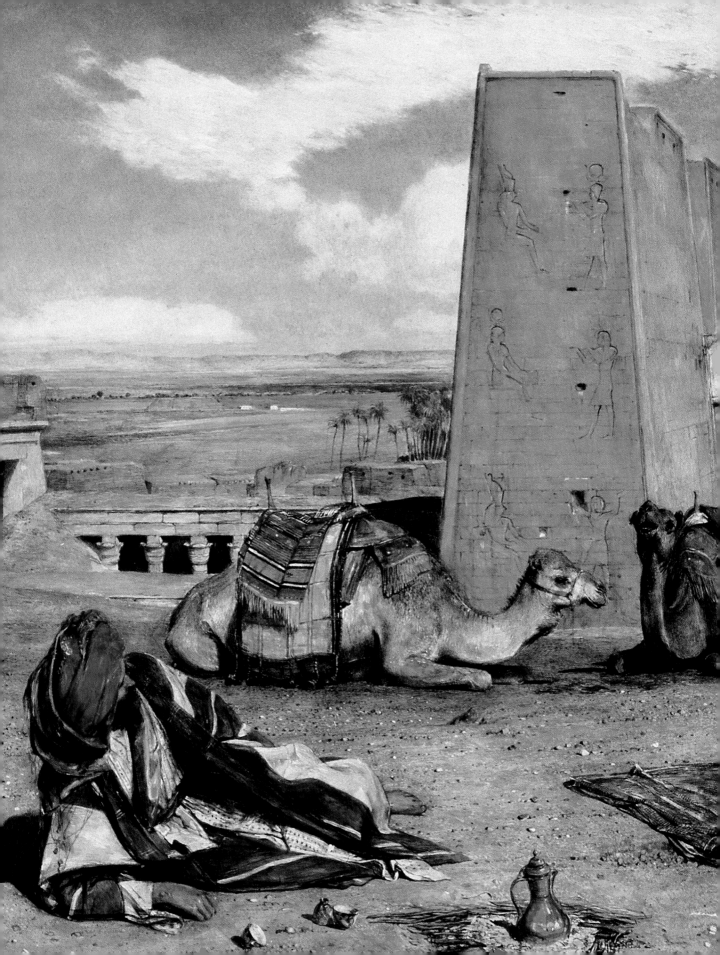

LIFE IN
THE MEDIEVAL MUSLIM WORLD

The Countryside

KATHRYN HINDS

MARSHALL CAVENDISH BENCHMARK NEW YORK

To Maria

The author and publishers wish to extend heartfelt thanks to Dr. Josef W. Meri, Fellow and Special Scholar in Residence, Royal Aal al-Bayt Institute for Islamic Thought, Amman, Jordan, for his gracious and invaluable assistance in reviewing the manuscript of this book.

MARSHALL CAVENDISH BENCHMARK 99 WHITE PLAINS ROAD TARRYTOWN, NEW YORK 10591 www.marshallcavendish.us Text copyright © 2009 by Marshall Cavendish Corporation. Map copyright © 2009 by Mike Reagan. All rights reserved. No part of this book may be reproduced or utilized in any form or by any means electronic or mechanical including photocopying, recording, or by any information storage and retrieval system, without permission from the copyright holders. All Internet sites were available and accurate when this book was sent to press. LIBRARY OF CONGRESS CATALOGING-IN-PUBLICATION DATA Hinds, Kathryn, 1962- The countryside / by Kathryn Hinds. p. cm. — (Life in the medieval Muslim world) Includes bibliographical references and index. Summary: "A social history of the Islamic world from the eighth through the mid-thirteenth century, with a focus on life in the desert and countryside"— Provided by publisher. ISBN 978-0-7614-3091-9 1. Islamic countries—Juvenile literature. 2. Deserts—Islamic countries—Social life and customs—Juvenile literature. I. Title. DS36.6.H564 2008 909'.0976701—dc22 2008019266

EDITOR: Joyce Needleman Stanton   PUBLISHER: Michelle Bisson
ART DIRECTOR: Anahid Hamparian   SERIES DESIGNER: Kristen Branch / Michael Nelson Design

Images provided by Rose Corbett Gordon and Alexandra (Sasha) Gordon, Art Editors of Mystic CT, from the following sources: Cover: Private Collection, © Whitford & Hughes, London/Bridgeman Art Library Back cover: (detail) The Metropolitan Museum of Art/Art Resource, NY Page 1: Borromeo/Art Resource, NY; pages 2-3, 12: The Tate Gallery, London/Art Resource, NY; pages 6, 45: Historical Picture Archive/Corbis; page 10: HIP/British Library/Art Resource, NY; page 11: The Art Archive/Turkish and Islamic Art Museum Istanbul/Alfredo Dagli Orti; pages 14, 34: Werner Forman/Art Resource, NY; page 16: The Art Archive/Stephanie Colasanti; page 17: Alinari Archives/The Image Works; page 18: Werner Forman/Topham/The Image Works; page 21: Bibliotheque des Arts Decoratifs, Paris, Archives Charmet/Bridgeman Art Library; page 23: Private Collection, © Portal Gallery Ltd/Bridgeman Art Library; pages 24, 70-71: Private Collection/Bridgeman Art Library; page 26: Brooklyn Museum of Art, New York, Purchased by special subscription/Bridgeman Art Library; page 29: Gérard Degeorge/Corbis; page 31: Victoria & Albert Museum/Art Resource, NY; page 32: Art Gallery of New South Wales, Sydney, Australia,/Bridgeman Art Library; page 36: Private Collection, © Whitford & Hughes, London/Bridgeman Art Library; page 38: The Art Archive/Musée Condé Chantilly/Gianni Dagli Orti; pages 40-41, 53: Private Collection, © The Fine Art Society, London/Bridgeman Art Library; pages 42-43: © Russell-Cotes Art Gallery and Museum, Bournemouth, UK/Bridgeman Art Library; page 47: Collection of Andrew McIntosh Patrick, UK/Bridgeman Art Library; page 49: Erich Lessing/Art Resource, NY; page 50: Leamington Spa Art Gallery & Museum/Bridgeman Art Library; page 55: Musee Conde, Chantilly, France, Giraudon/Bridgeman Art Library; pages 56, 84: Art Resource, NY; page 58: Private Collection, The Stapleton Collection/Bridgeman Art Library; pages 60, 82-83 Fine Art Photographic Library/Corbis; page 62: Private Collection, Photo © Bonhams, London/Bridgeman Art Library; page 64: The Art Archive/Musée du Louvre Paris/Gianni Dagli Orti; pages 67, 76: The Art Archive/National Library Cairo/Gianni Dagli Orti; page 68: Private Collection, Photo © Christie's Images/Bridgeman Art Library; page 73: Ecole Nationale des Langues Orientales, Paris, Archives Charmet/Bridgeman Art Library; page 74: (detail) The Metropolitan Museum of Art/Art Resource, NY; page 78: AISA Media, Barcelona; page 81: Lindley Library, RHS, London/Bridgeman Art Library; page 86: British Museum, London/Bridgeman Art Library; page 87: British Library, London© British Library Board. All Rights Reserved/ Bridgeman Art Library.

Printed in China
135642

front cover: Many nineteenth-century European artists enjoyed depicting Middle Eastern scenes like this one of herders leading their goats to a water source at the desert's edge.

half-title page: A gazelle pictured in a manuscript from Muslim-ruled northern India

title page: A caravan rests among ancient Egyptian ruins in a painting by British artist John Frederick Lewis.

back cover: A man strains honey in the shade of his fruit trees. This illustration is from a thirteenth-century Iraqi manuscript.

Contents

About the Medieval Muslim World

IN THE YEAR 622 AN ARABIAN MERCHANT NAMED Muhammad, accompanied by two hundred followers, left his home city of Mecca for the troubled town of Yathrib. Its citizens knew that Muhammad had been receiving visions from God and preaching what God had revealed to him. His message was unpopular in Mecca, but the people of Yathrib welcomed Muhammad to be their chief judge and embraced his teaching of Islam, or submission to God. They recognized Muhammad as the Prophet of God, and their city soon became known as Madinat al-Nabi, "City of the Prophet," or simply Medina.

The Hegira, Muhammad's move to Medina, marked the beginning of the Islamic community, the *umma*. From that point on, the community of Muslims (followers of Islam) grew rapidly. By 634 it embraced the entire Arabian Peninsula. By 750 Muslim rulers controlled a wide band of territory from the Iberian Peninsula, across North Africa, to the borders of India. During the following centuries the *umma* continued to expand into India, Anatolia (modern Turkey), Central Asia, and sub-Saharan Africa. Along the way, Arab

Opposite: The Great Mosque of Mecca. Draped in black cloth in the center of the courtyard is the Kaaba, which was a holy place even before the coming of Islam.

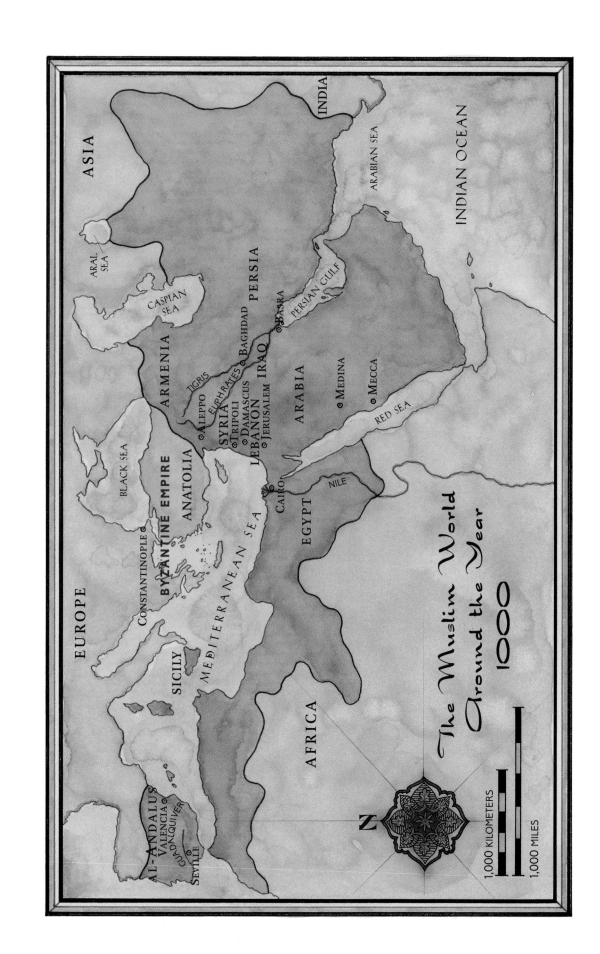

The Muslim World Around the Year 1000

and local cultures mingled and sometimes melded, leading to the development of a shared culture with many ways of expressing itself.

The Dar al-Islam, "Abode of Islam," was politically united for only a brief period. But it remained united in other important ways, through religious beliefs and language. Arabic, the language of the Qur'an (the holy book of Islam), became the common tongue of nearly all Muslims in Islam's early centuries. In most areas it was used not just in religion but also in government, law, literature, and learning. This meant that no matter where a Muslim went in the Dar al-Islam, he or she would be able to share news and knowledge with other Muslims. In fact the gathering, communication, and spreading of knowledge and skills in the arts and sciences was one of the great achievements of the Muslim world during this era. For this reason, it is often referred to as the Golden Age of Islam. In the history of the West, this time is generally called the Middle Ages, and for convenience we use both that term and *medieval* for this period even when discussing areas outside Europe.

The Dar al-Islam and Christian medieval Europe often conflicted with each other. Yet there was also a great deal of peaceful interchange between the two, in many ways to the lasting benefit of European civilization. And at various times and places in the medieval Muslim world, Muslims, Christians, and Jews lived and worked side by side in an atmosphere of tolerance seldom found elsewhere in the past. In the present, too, we can find much to learn from both the successes and the struggles of the Dar al-Islam in the Middle Ages.

This series of books looks at the lives of the people who lived in that diverse world, focusing mainly on the Middle East and Muslim Spain in the eighth through thirteenth centuries. In this volume we will meet the people of the medieval Muslim world's countryside:

About the Medieval Muslim World

A worship service in a synagogue built in Muslim-ruled Spain. Under Islam, Jews enjoyed a higher level of religious freedom and civil rights than they had known in most Christian states.

farmers and herders, villagers and nomads, housewives and country gentlemen. We will visit their homes and discover the sights, sounds, and smells that surrounded rural people. We will see what kinds of work they did, how they relaxed, and how they coped with life's hardships. So step back into history, to a time of faith and intellect, intrigue and excitement, struggle and splendor. Welcome to life in the medieval Muslim world!

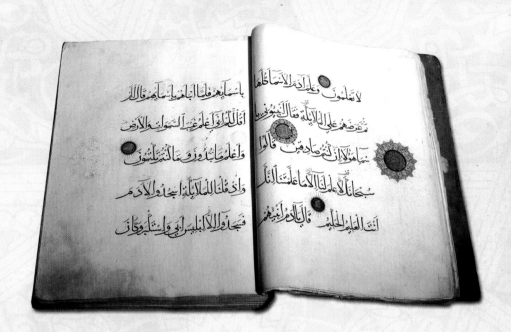

A NOTE ON DATES AND NAMES

For Muslims the Hegira (Arabic *hijra*, "departure" or "migration") began a new age and so became the year 1 of the Muslim calendar. Dates in this calendar are labeled AH, for *Anno Hegira*, or simply H. For ease of reading, though, this series of books uses the conventional Western dating system. Also for ease of reading, we are using the common Westernized forms of many Arabic names—for example, *Avicenna* instead of *Ibn Sina*—and we are leaving out most of the special accent marks that scholars use when converting Arabic names to the Western alphabet. There are many different ways to convert Arabic to English, especially because the Arabic alphabet does not include symbols for most vowels. For this reason, you may see the same names spelled slightly different ways in different books. In many sources you may also see the God of Islam referred to as Allah. Since the Arabic word *Allah* simply means *God* and refers to the same deity worshiped by Jews and Christians, we have chosen to use *God* instead of *Allah* in this series.

Above: A Qur'an from thirteenth-century Persia, written in flowing Arabic script

City and country were closely connected, with farmland often lying just outside a city's walls. In this painting from the 1850s, orchards and pastures extend right up to the medieval wall surrounding Jerusalem.

ONE

Life on the Land

*Since agriculture is at the basis of civilization the whole of life and its
principal advantages depend upon it.*

➤➤IBN ABDUN, TWELFTH-CENTURY MARKET INSPECTOR IN SEVILLE

THE MEDIEVAL MUSLIM WORLD IS LARGELY KNOWN
for the refined and elegant life of its palaces and cities—the
poetry and music, the fine craftsmanship that turned everyday
objects into works of art, the learned discussions of both the
Qur'an and ancient Greek philosophy, the striving after scientific
knowledge, and so on. Yet, as in every place before the modern age,
most of the people of the Dar al-Islam lived in the countryside. It
was their labor and the abundance they brought from the land that
laid the foundations of the medieval Muslim world's prosperity and
splendid civilization.

At the same time, the strong governments of Muslim rulers
brought stability, efficient administration, and profitable trade to

many regions that had not enjoyed such advantages for centuries. In addition, the Muslim thirst for learning led scientists to make detailed studies of plants, animals, soil types, fertilizers, and irrigation techniques; to exchange their information with other researchers; and to record their findings in books on agriculture,

A tenth-century manuscript from Central Asia containing descriptions and illustrations of a variety of plants, especially those used for medicines. This page is devoted to the tree that produced frankincense, which grew only in southern Arabia and eastern Africa.

which could be found in the libraries of every significant town. All these factors combined to enable farmers to bring more land under cultivation, to adopt more efficient farming methods, to expand the range of crops they grew, and to find more markets for their surplus produce. Muslim rule brought with it an agricultural revolution that benefitted everyone.

EARTH AND WATER

The Dar al-Islam stretched from the Atlantic Ocean to the Indian Ocean and half encircled the Mediterranean Sea. This vast territory encompassed a variety of terrains, including seacoasts, river valleys, mountains, deserts, and plains. Climate varied widely from region to region. Throughout the Islamic world, June through August were the hottest months, and January the coldest. But the difference between summer and winter temperatures, or even between daytime and nighttime temperatures, was much greater in inland areas than on the seacoasts.

Coastal areas were damp and humid; plains and, of course, deserts were quite dry. There were areas where almost no rain fell (such as Egypt), while in southern Arabia monsoon winds brought months of downpours. Summer was the season of the monsoons; in areas untouched by these tropical winds, autumn and winter tended to bring the most rainfall. In some places, the rains filled riverbeds that would be nothing but dry gullies in the hot months. Where there was little or no rainfall, or it was unpredictable from year to year, people and animals depended on wells, springs, or rivers for their water.

The three great rivers of the Middle East—the Nile, Tigris, and Euphrates—flooded every year. The Tigris and Euphrates floods occurred in springtime, fed by melting snows in the mountains of

Windswept desert dunes in North Africa almost hide the greenery of an oasis.

Anatolia. The Nile's flood resulted from the heavy spring rains in the east African highlands, where the river had its sources. By June or July, Egypt would see the Nile's level rising till it overflowed the banks and covered the low-lying land for as much as five miles on either side. With all three rivers, the floodwaters were channeled into networks of canals and ponds, to be used for watering crops during the dry growing season.

Canal networks were among a variety of irrigation systems used in the medieval Muslim world. Water was regarded as a precious resource: its use was carefully regulated, and there were laws against wasting it. In al-Andalus (the Arabic name for Muslim Spain), water was sent through irrigation canals multiple times, and the canal outlets were adapted to the different types of soil they fed. Everywhere rainwater was collected and stored in holding tanks and

The Countryside

reservoirs. To protect springwater from waste through evaporation, it was often channeled through underground tunnels called *qanats*. These conduits used a gentle downhill slope, allowing gravity to get the water from its source to its outlet—often a distance of many, many miles. Some scholars estimate that, before modern times, 70 percent of Persia's water was channeled through *qanats*—a total of around 100,000 miles of them.

The Nile River in full flood, bringing water and fertility to farmland at the desert's edge

Terrain, weather patterns, and water supply worked together to affect the soil. The Nile, Tigris, and Euphrates floods brought not only water but also layers of silt, rich earth that renewed the fertility of the land. Very productive ground was also found in coastal plains and the sea-facing slopes of hills and mountains. In the mountains, however, it was necessary to terrace the land to prevent the good soil from being washed away by the rain. Inland areas tended to

"Bright strands of water" stream off a *noria* in Hama, Syria, where such waterwheels have been in constant use since the Middle Ages.

In Praise of the Waterwheel

For efficient irrigation of water-hungry crops, it was often necessary to raise water up from its source to flow into the channels that would convey it to the fields. A number of devices were used for this, some of them dating back to ancient times. Probably the most common water-raising machine, though, was one developed and perfected by Muslim engineers. This was a type of waterwheel known as the *noria*. It was used abundantly almost everywhere in the medieval Muslim world—there were eight thousand of them in and around the Andalusian city of Valencia alone—and *norias* are still employed in parts of Spain and the Middle East today. *Norias* were graceful machines, so admired for their beauty as well as their efficiency that even poets praised them. Abu Abd-Allah ben Abi-l-Husain, an official in North Africa, wrote this poem about a *noria* around 1240:

> Round-shouldered, towards the earth inclined,
> It waters the dust with glistening pearls.
> Like a singing bow, its upper half
> Shoots streams of water all around
> Like the spheres of heaven, for its gushings
> Are like shooting stars, fighting the earth's aridity [dryness].
> A juggler, entranced by the dancing of the branches,
> Strikes the wheel with naked swords.
> I do not believe thirst makes it sigh
> Since the waters flow over its shoulders.
> It is really a singer and the garden a drinker,
> And the drink and the song are eternally bound.
> The bright strands of water against the dark wood
> Stand out like bright gifts against the darkness of requests.

have thinner soil, but it was still fertile. Many plains, though, along with mountain slopes facing away from the sea, had poor, dry, rocky ground. And deserts varied from places where only a few scrubby plants could grow to expanses of rock and gravel to seas of sand dunes. Yet even in the midst of deserts, underground springs often welled up to form oases, islands of water and greenery.

CROPS AND FLOCKS

The type of land and availability of water determined what kinds of crops and livestock people could raise. There were three major crops in the Dar al-Islam: grain, dates, and olives. In general, the richest soil and most abundant water were necessary for growing wheat, rice, and other grains. Thanks to the Nile floods, Egypt was the greatest grain-producing country in the Mediterranean region, as it had been since ancient times. The Tigris and Euphrates valleys also grew ample grain, and were home to lush groves of date palms as well.

Dates could grow in less well-watered places, too, such as oases, but they wouldn't produce fruit where temperatures dipped below 61 degrees Fahrenheit (16 degrees Celsius). Olives—highly valued for themselves and for their oil, which was used for cooking, cosmetics, and as lamp fuel—had moderate requirements. Needing less rain than grains and able to handle a range of temperatures and a variety of soils, olives grew abundantly in al-Andalus and on the coastal plains of North Africa.

The farmers of the medieval Muslim world raised a great assortment of fruits and vegetables. Thanks to the thriving network of trade that was fostered by shared language and culture, useful plants native to one area could be found growing throughout the Dar al-Islam. Trade also helped spread plants from farther away—for example, rice from China, almonds from Central Asia, and

Dates ripen in a palm tree beside the Nile River.

Life on the Land

cotton, oranges, and sugarcane from India. Among the many kinds of fruits and vegetables cultivated were figs, grapes, apples, apricots, cherries, bananas, mangos, melons, lemons, pomegranates, mulberries, walnuts, pine nuts, pistachios, eggplants, artichokes, onions, spinach, radishes, carrots, cucumbers, turnips, lentils, and fava beans. Mint, tarragon, coriander, basil, thyme, garlic, and numerous other herbs were grown for the flavor they could add to foods as well as for their medicinal properties. Fiber production was important, too, and farmers raised cotton, linen, hemp, and silkworms, as well as dye plants such as indigo and henna.

Wool was another vital material, and flocks of sheep could be found throughout the Islamic world. Some of the finest wool came from specially bred sheep raised in the western parts of North Africa. (These were probably the ancestors of Spanish merino sheep, still the source of a very soft wool prized by knitters and the garment industry.) Arabia, on the other hand, was famous for breeding exceptional horses. Arabia was also known for producing the best camels for carrying loads across the deserts. For any given domestic animal, livestock breeders had access to varieties from all over the Islamic world and were able to select for the best qualities and develop superior breeds.

Animals were raised for different purposes. Sheep provided not only wool but also meat and milk. Goats and cows, too, were kept for meat and milk (cows, however—also the main source of leather—required richer land for grazing than goats and sheep did). Camels could supply wool, meat, and milk but were most valued as beasts of burden, especially for long overland journeys through dry areas. In other places and circumstances, donkeys were the usual transport (besides walking), while horses were mainly ridden by the wealthy. Wheeled vehicles were rare in the medieval Muslim world,

Fig Smuggling

Many new crops were acquired through trade, while others were spread by travelers who obtained seeds or cuttings of plants to take home with them. Sometimes these travelers were acting under the orders of rulers, sometimes under their own initiative. And sometimes they resorted to devious tactics to get the plants they wanted. One source, for example, relates this story about a ninth-century Andalusian traveler:

The doñegal variety of fig was introduced by al-Ghazal when he went from Córdoba to Constantinople as an envoy. He saw that fig there and admired it. It was forbidden to take anything from Constantinople. He took the green fig [apparently a seedling is meant] and concealed it among his books that he had wrapped up. When he took his leave he was searched but no sign was found of it. When he arrived in Córdoba he removed the plant from the wrappings, planted it and tended it. When it bore fruit he took it and presented it to the lord of Córdoba. He told him about his ruse in procuring it and his lord thanked him.

Above: Fresh or dried, figs were a sweet treat for rich and poor alike, especially in places where dates would not grow.

Camels were the best form of transport across desert areas.

so animals were seldom needed to pull carts. Oxen, though, and sometimes camels or donkeys, were employed in pulling plows, turning waterwheels, drawing water from wells, and other farm-work. All farm animals further contributed to rural productivity by providing manure, which was used as fertilizer.*

In addition to its fields and flocks, the countryside was endowed with other resources that enriched the medieval Muslim world. There might be wild game, hunted for meat, skins, and sport. Some areas produced timber, such as the renowned cedar trees of Lebanon. In some places clay could be dug, to be made into pots, tiles, and other

*Muslim farmers did not raise pigs because Muslim law, like Jewish law, forbade the eating of pork. But pigs continued to be raised by some Christian farmers in Muslim-ruled lands.

The Countryside

ceramics. Mineral resources included chemicals (for dyestuffs and medicines), silicon sand (for glassmaking), building stone, metals, and gems and semiprecious stones. Many regions were blessed with a variety of rural abundance. So Hisdai ibn Shaprut, the Jewish physician and vizier to the ruler of al-Andalus in the mid-900s, described the rich resources of the countryside around Córdoba:

> It is a land of grains, wines, and purest oils, rich in plants, a paradise of every sort of sweet. And with gardens and orchards where every kind of fruit tree blossoms, and those with silkworms in their leaves. . . . Our land also has its own sources of silver and gold and in her mountains we mine copper and iron, tin and lead, kohl and marble and crystal.

TWO

Country Communities

Have you seen the villages the kings have planted
When their fields are green
Surrounded by vineyards, palm trees
And fragrant herbs from which the birds take their seeds?

↠KHURAYMI, NINTH-CENTURY IRAQI POET

ISLAM WAS BORN IN A LAND WHERE FAMILY connections were the most important of all bonds. When Muhammad began his teachings in Mecca and Medina, most of Arabia lacked government institutions that would look after people's interests. Instead it was the extended family, or clan, that guaranteed protection, support, and justice. For example, a child whose parents died would be raised by another clan member (as the orphaned Muhammad was adopted by his father's brother), and a widow would often be married to one of her dead husband's relatives. If some of a man's livestock were stolen, the other men of his clan were expected to help him get the animals back and punish the

Opposite: Painted in Syria around 1905 by American artist John Singer Sargent, these Bedouin nomads lived and dressed much as their medieval ancestors did.

thieves (usually by taking a number of their animals). If someone was killed, his or her clan took vengeance, even to the extent of going to war against the killer's clan; the less honorable (but sometimes necessary) alternative to avenging the death was to accept the compensation of "blood money" from the other clan.

A number of clans together made up a tribe; its members all regarded themselves as descended from the same male ancestor. The tribe offered protection against larger threats, such as during times of war. And members of the same tribe expected to receive hospitality and assistance from one another. This made travel and trade much safer and easier for people, since a tribe often had member clans living in a number of places—a person or family could travel a long way from home, knowing that they could expect help from their tribe if they needed it.

Clan and tribal bonds have remained important in much of Muslim society through history. But Muhammad also created another kind of bond: that of fellow believers. Ideally, the *umma* was united as a spiritual family, and the ties of spiritual kinship surpassed those of blood kinship. In other words, the *umma* could be thought of as a single tribe, with membership in it erasing all other divisions between Muslims. In reality, conflicts between different family groups arose almost immediately after Muhammad's death. Nevertheless, the concept of a community of believers united in spite of their differences has remained a powerful ideal.

THE VILLAGE

Country dwellers generally identified themselves in terms of their religion and their kin. In addition to these bonds of faith and family, people also had a strong sense of belonging to their local community—their village or neighborhood. It was necessary to

The Countryside

work with other community members to make the most of the available water and land. This cooperation extended across religious barriers, as many villages were home to both Muslims and Christians, and sometimes Jews as well. In al-Andalus and elsewhere, members of the different faiths shared the land and water, as well as facilities such as bathhouses, community ovens, and the mills where grain was ground into flour.

Where irrigation was used, there were a variety of arrangements for sharing water. For instance, farmers might be able to draw water only from a certain assigned section of a canal or stream. Sometimes water clocks were attached to sluice gates, mechanically opening and shutting them to direct the water into different channels. Or a water clock might be used to time each farmer's water

A canal brings water from the river to outlying areas of Basra, Iraq.

usage, with farmers taking scheduled turns to irrigate their fields. People who broke the water regulations could be brought before a court called the Tribunal of the Waters. It met at the community's main mosque, and its judges were chosen by the local farmers.

In some places the village's fields were divided up among the farming families in a different way each year, or redistributed every few years, so that over the long run everyone would share equally in the benefits of the best land and the challenges of working the poorer land. In other places families cultivated the same land year after year, generation after generation. Many farmers were sharecroppers, working land that was owned by someone else. The owner supplied seeds, and the farmer planted them, cared for the growing crop, and then harvested it. The farmer kept half the harvest and gave the other half to the owner, who might also be entitled to one of the farmer's sheep in return for use of the land. If the owner supplied not only seed but also work animals and tools (such as a plow and the oxen to pull it), the farmer might only keep as little as one-quarter of the harvest. Even so, the arrangement could be as beneficial to landless families as it was to owners who couldn't work all their land themselves, and sharecropping contracts often had terms of many years.

Farmlands usually surrounded the village where the farmers lived. Some villages were protected by high mud-brick walls. The houses, too, were generally built of mud-brick, called *al-tub* (from which we get the word *adobe*), or occasionally of stone. In many areas, though, some peasant dwellings were little more than huts constructed of reeds. Families who were better off would naturally have more substantial homes, often with several rooms arranged around a courtyard.

Like houses, villages varied in size, but they could be relatively large. A census of Egypt in the eighth century indicates that the typical village there was home to at least five hundred farm families.

Indeed, agricultural land was densely populated throughout the medieval Muslim world. For example, in al-Andalus there were an estimated 12,000 villages along the Guadalquivir River alone. And along the Tigris River in Iraq, it was said that the villages were so close together that in the morning the crowing roosters called to one another from Baghdad all the way down to Basra, near the river's outlet into the Persian Gulf.

A traveler passes the heat of the day resting in the shade of an adobe house.

TOWN AND COUNTRY

The countryside was dotted with market towns, conveniently located where two or more farming districts met. The average market town seems to have been smaller than the average village—many market towns had only a few hundred residents. Some of the townspeople might go out every day to work in the

A horse market in Syria, depicted by a nineteenth-century Italian artist. Fine horses were a status symbol for the wealthy. The Bedouin also prized horses for their abilities in battle.

nearby fields, but a large percentage of the residents were merchants and craftspeople. They did business with the farmers who brought their surplus produce and livestock into town and sold or bartered it for the things they could not grow or make themselves.

Business was conducted on an even larger scale in the cities of the medieval Muslim world. For example, merchants in the Syrian city of Aleppo bought fruit from the orchards and forests to the north, grain from the plains to the east, sheep from the surrounding hills, and camels from the desert to the south. Much of this produce was resold and sent elsewhere, for Aleppo, located on the main route from Syria to Anatolia, was a great trade center.

Cities had close ties with the surrounding countryside, which was generally under their government. This made sense, since the countryside supplied the city people with food and various raw materials (cotton, wool, leather, wood, etc.), which they needed for their crafts and trades as well as for their sustenance. The countryside was rarely far away: farms and orchards might even lie right outside the city walls. This is the impression we get from reading Persian traveler Nasr-i Khusraw's description of one of the cities he visited in what is now Lebanon: "The whole neighborhood of [Tripoli] is occupied by fields, and gardens, and trees. The sugar-cane grows here luxuriously, as likewise orange and citron trees; also the banana, the lemon, and the date."

Such lush rural scenes gave great pleasure to many city dwellers, who enjoyed getting away from the urban noise and bustle when they could. Wealthy city people often had a house in the countryside, where they could go riding or hunting, relax in the garden, entertain friends, and simply enjoy the fresh air and sunshine. The rural environment impacted Muslim civilization in other ways, too: Scholars made studies of plants and animals; artists and architects took inspiration from trees and flowers. Poets composed evocative descriptions of nature—doves and gazelles and horses, roses and running water, trees and fruits and vegetables. The twelfth-century Andalusian poet Ibn Quzman even wrote this amusing poem about the radish's tendency to make people burp after eating it:

> The radish is a good
> And doubtless wholesome food,
> But proves, to vex the eater,
> A powerful repeater.
>
> This only fault I find:
> What should be left behind
> Comes issuing instead
> Right from the eater's head!

CELEBRATING NATURE

Arabic poetry traditionally described landscapes, animals, and other aspects of the natural world mainly as a backdrop for the emotions expressed in the poems. But in the tenth century, writers began to appreciate and depict nature for its own sake, as in this piece by the Syrian poet Sanawbari.

> When there is fruit in the summer, the earth is aglow and the air shimmers with light.
> When in autumn the palm trees shed their leaves, naked is the earth, stark the air.
> And when in winter rain comes in endless torrent, the earth seems besieged and the air a captive.
> The only time is the time of the radiant spring, for it brings flowers and joy.
> Then the earth is a hyacinth, the air is a pearl, the plants turquoises, and the water crystal.

Above: Flowers were loved for their beauty and valued for their medicinal properties, too.
This illustration comes from a tenth-century Arabic translation of an ancient Greek medical book.

FOLLOWING THE FLOCKS

In Islam's original homeland, the Arabian Peninsula, much of the land was too dry for farming, and this was true of many of the other areas that came under Muslim rule. In such places, people lived a way of life that was thousands of years old, raising flocks of animals that they herded from place to place. A technical term for this lifestyle is nomadic pastoralism—*nomadic* refers to traveling or wandering, and *pastoralism* means caring for livestock.

The nomads of Arabia and neighboring areas were (and still are) known as the Bedouin, from Arabic *badawi*, meaning desert dweller. The Bedouin and other nomads did not, however, live among sand dunes, but in the semidesert areas where there were hardy grasses and other plants that required only small amounts of rain to thrive. This was where the nomads' camels, horses, and flocks of sheep and goats grazed. When there was no more food, the people took down the tents that were their homes, and they and their livestock moved on. As the ninth-century writer Ibn Qutayba explained, "the dwellers in tents were different from townsmen or villagers in respect of coming and going, because they moved from one water-spring to another, seeking pasture and searching out the places where rain had fallen."

The Bedouin lived in tight-knit tribal groups, in which they took great pride. This pride was well expressed by the Arab Christian poet Abd al-Malik in response to a woman who mocked his tribe for not being very large:

I answered her—Yea: the count of noble men is little.
But not few canst thou call those whose remnants are like to us
—young men who vie with the old in the quest of glory.
It hurts us naught that we be few, when our friend by us

The Bedouin settled down only briefly, moving on when their flocks had exhausted the available grazing land.

is safe, though the friends of most men beside be trampled. . . .
To the best of the Uplands we wend, and when the season comes,
we travel adown to the best of fruitful valleys.
Like rain of the heaven are we: there is not in all our line
one blunt of heart, nor among us is counted a niggard [miser].
We say nay whenso we will to the words of other men:
but no man to us says nay when we give sentence. . . .

Because the Bedouin were free (or freer than villagers and town dwellers) of control from outside the tribe, they regarded themselves as supremely noble and honorable. They often looked down on peasants as being people without liberty and on merchants and craftsmen—particularly traveling metalworkers, perfume sellers, and other peddlers—as being people without any tribe. Nevertheless, nomads had many interactions with merchants and craftworkers, who supplied such necessities as cooking pots and weapons. As for farmers, agriculture and the nomadic lifestyle were mutually beneficial. Nomads needed grain, fruits, and vegetables; villagers and townspeople needed livestock, leather, meat, and wool. In many cases there were long-standing trading relationships between nomadic groups and the oasis farmers of the regions they traveled.

THREE

Men of the Soil

I used to have a little farm
which gave me what I needed every year.

↠ Ubayd-i Zakani, fourteenth-century Persian poet

MONG BOTH FARMERS AND NOMADS, THE
typical rural household consisted of three generations:
children, parents, and paternal grandparents. Family relationships were nearly always traced through the father's side of the
family. For this reason a clan or tribe was generally known as the
"sons of" their ancestor—Muhammad's clan, for example, was the
Banu Hashim, the Sons of Hashim (the Prophet's grandfather).
Normally the oldest male was the head of the family.

In farming communities, the heads of families were the village
elders. The elders helped settle disputes between villagers and made
decisions on issues that affected the well-being of the community

Opposite: Elders hold a council while behind them other men practice horsemanship or tend the
tribe's livestock. Since this painting comes from the 1800s, the elders are armed with rifles as
well as the more traditional swords and daggers.

as a whole. In nomadic groups, too, the elders had an influential and authoritative role. The head of the most prominent family in a tribe was often known as the *shaykh* (Arabic for "old man"). He was looked to for leadership but could not necessarily force tribe members to do anything. His power was the power of persuasion, which he earned because of his reputation for courage, honor, and generosity.

WORKING WITH THE SEASONS

In Islamic society, a man was expected to be the provider for his family. For most men, this meant working on the land in one way or another. What a man did from day to day, though, could vary greatly depending on the weather and the seasons. If he raised livestock, he

After visiting Egypt in the 1880s, Scottish artist Joseph Farquharson painted this scene of shepherds and their flock beside the Nile.

had to take the animals' life cycles into account, too. To increase his flocks and herds, he could just let nature take its course during the mating season. But if he wanted to breed stock with particular characteristics, he would have to match up animals likely to pass on those traits. Then, when it was time for the baby animals to be born, both mothers and babies might need extra care—most farmers and herders had to act as their own veterinarians if anything went wrong. Female animals might also need special attention if they were going to be milked in addition to nursing their offspring.

As we have seen, nomadic pastoralists took their livestock from place to place to make the best of the sparse vegetation in dry regions. Settled farmers, too, moved their flocks in many cases. They would

drive the animals into the hills to graze during the summer, then bring them back down to their lowland pastures for the winter. This system of seasonal herding is technically known as transhumance, and it could be practiced in different ways. In some cases the entire community migrated with the animals; in others the animals were accompanied only by shepherds, while the rest of the community stayed in one place, tending the fields and gardens and orchards.

The territory under Muslim rule was so large, and so diverse in geography and climate, that the timing of farm tasks varied a good bit from region to region. The basic work, however, remained the same: plowing and fertilizing the fields, sowing the seeds, tending and weeding around the growing plants, and bringing in the har-

With the Nile's floodwaters receding, it will soon be time for farmers to plant their crops.

vest. In Egypt and Iraq, these tasks followed the rhythm of the rivers' flooding, as they had for thousands of years.

In Egypt, the Nile's waters covered the land from June or July to September or October. As the grain fields dried out, farmers cleared the irrigation canals and ditches, then plowed and hoed the soil. Plowing was long hard work, even with oxen or other draft animals to pull the plow. The farmer had to steer it, pushing down on it the whole time so that it cut into the earth properly. After this, the farmer sowed seeds in the plowed furrows, then drove his draft animals over the field to press the seeds into the ground.

The whole time the grain was growing, the farmer had to assure that it was getting enough water. He was constantly tending to the

Men of the Soil

irrigation channels and raising water up from them to pour onto the fields. He kept this up till harvest season, which in Egypt generally began in February and lasted through May, since different crops ripened at different times. To harvest the grain, the farmer (usually with the help of family members or hired laborers) walked up and down the field, grabbing several stalks with one hand and cutting them with a sickle held in his other hand.

The cut grain was loaded into baskets carried by donkeys, who took it to be threshed. This was often done by spreading it out on the threshing floor and having oxen walk over it to break the grain apart from the stalks. The next step was winnowing, which separated the grain from the chaff, the remaining bits of stalk and husk. One of the easiest ways to do this was to put the threshed grain into a big shallow basket and toss the grain a little way into the air, allowing the wind to blow away the chaff. Then the grain could finally be stored, or shipped off for sale in city markets.

The agricultural cycle followed a different rhythm elsewhere. In al-Andalus, for instance, grain was planted in January—which was the month for harvesting sugarcane, too. January and February were also when farmers put in stakes for olive and pomegranate trees, set up trellises for vining plants, grafted apple and pear trees, and planted saplings. By May, ears of wheat were forming; in July they were ready for harvest. A tenth-century document known as the Calendar of Córdoba lists a variety of agricultural activities for July:

> Amongst the events of the month . . . are the following: the harvesting of the wheat and the threshing of the barley. The grapes ripen and the pistachios begin to form, the sugary pears and the sharp-tasting apples are ready. Marrow jam, pear and apple syrups are made. The bulk of the grapes ripen and the harvest

SPRINGTIME IN AL-ANDALUS

The Calendar of Córdoba was written by a Christian bishop named Rabi ben Zaid, also known as Recemund. Like numerous other Andalusian Christians, Rabi had adopted many aspects of the culture spread by Muslim rulers, including the Arabic language. His calendar was basically an almanac, listing the holidays, identifying the constellations, noting the times of sunrise and sunset, and describing the agricultural tasks for each month of the year. Composed in Arabic, the calendar was dedicated to the ruler of al-Andalus, who ordered Latin translations of it sent to Germany, Constantinople, and Jerusalem. Here is Rabi's description of life on the land in the month of March:

In March fig trees are grafted. The young shoots appear, and most of the trees burst into leaf. The falcons of Valencia lay eggs on the islands, and incubate them for thirty days. Sugar cane is planted. The first roses and lilies come into flower. Garden beans begin to ripen. Quails appear. The silkworms emerge. Sturgeon and shad leave the sea and swim upriver. Cucumbers are planted, cotton sown, garden crocus, eggplant, mint and marjoram . . . This is the month when letters are sent to managers for the purchase of horses for the princes. Swarms of young locusts begin to migrate, and they must be destroyed quickly. . . .

Above: Partridges were birds that country people looked to as a source of food.

is assessed. The following medicinal herbs are gathered: mustard, nigella, thyme and marshmallow. Small partridge appear and are hunted. Figs are dried in the plains.

According to the Calendar of Córdoba, every month was just as busy as July. It was constant work to wrest a living from the earth.

DEFENDING TRIBE AND LAND

The Bedouin and other nomads were not tied to any one piece of land. Their wealth and property came not from fields and crops but from flocks and herds. A nomadic community had a certain territory that it ranged through, but this territory might overlap with that of other groups. Because resources were scarce in semidesert areas, conflicts could arise between competing tribes who might want to use the same water sources or pastures. In addition, Bedouin men had a long-standing tradition of conducting *razzias*, or raids, to capture livestock from rival groups. One of a man's chief duties, therefore, was to always be ready and able to fight for his tribe, whether to defend it or to gain more wealth for it.

In a lament for her dead brother, "Sakhr the generous, . . . who led his tribe before he grew a beard," the seventh-century Arabian poet al-Khansa described some of the qualities of an ideal Bedouin man:

. . . to him we looked for protection and strength,
who in winter's blast would see none want,
nor keep to his tent to husband stores
but set his board at the bite of cold,
ready his welcome, with open hand,
a heart so quick to command in need.

British traveler and scholar Sir Richard Francis Burton admired the noble qualities of the Beduoin and had himself portrayed in traditional Arab dress in this picture made in 1854. Burton was fluent in Arabic and immersed himself in Arab culture. He made the first English translation of *The Arabian Nights* and, although not a Muslim, he made pilgrimages to Mecca and Medina.

Men of the Soil

No woman, alone, saw him ever set foot
in any but honourable quest. . . .

In addition to generosity and respect toward women, Sakhr demonstrated the bravery and warrior spirit that were expected of a Bedouin man:

When men stretched out their hands
in battle, in quest of honor
competing to excel—he came, stretched out a hand,
and reached the glory that was beyond their reach.
He brought them what raised them up
though he was the youngest of them in years.

War was part of the lives of many landowners, too. Usama ibn Munqidh (1095–1188) belonged to a noble family who lived on an estate in Syria during the time when Christian Crusaders conquered and held Jerusalem and other parts of what are now Israel, Palestine, Lebanon, and Syria. In his old age, Usama wrote a book in which he recalled a variety of incidents in his and his family's lives. His father, he wrote, "was greatly addicted to warfare. His body bore scars of terrible wounds." On one occasion, "he was hit with an arrow in his leg. In his slipper he had a dagger. The arrow struck the dagger and was broken on it, without even wounding him—thanks to the excellent protection of Allah (exalted is he!)."

Usama himself fought his first battle against the Crusaders (or Franks, as Muslims referred to them) when he was twenty-four. Telling his father about the fight afterward, he said, "The moment I saw that the Franks were in contact with our men, then I felt that death would be an easy matter for me. So I turned back to the

An illustration from a fourteenth-century Italian manuscript shows Crusaders besieging Jerusalem.

Franks, either to be killed or to protect that crowd [of Muslims]."
His father then praised him by quoting this verse:

> The coward among men flees precipitately before danger
>   facing his own mother,
> But the brave one protects even him whom it is not his duty
>   to shelter.

Men of the Soil

Women and men were both expected to dress modestly, but women often wore extra coverings when they went out in public, to shield themselves from strangers' eyes.

FOUR

Rural Women

No one can deny magnanimity, enthusiasm and sound judgment in the case of noble women.

→ USAMA IBN MUNQIDH, TWELFTH-CENTURY SYRIAN GENTLEMAN AND WRITER

FULFILLING HIS DUTY TO PROTECT HIS FAMILY was part of a man's honor. For a woman, honor lay in safeguarding the family's purity. An honorable woman had no relationships with men she was not related to. If she had to interact with men from outside the family for any reason, she was careful to dress and behave with extreme modesty. In some situations women's concern for the family honor could take dramatic forms. For example, one time when Usama ibn Munqidh and the other men of his family were away fighting an enemy, his mother had to take charge of defending their home. She passed out all the available weapons to any servants able to wield them, then beckoned Usama's sister and led her to the balcony of the house. Usama

51

returned not long afterward and asked what his sister was doing there. His mother answered,

> "O my dear son, I have given her a seat at the balcony and sat behind her so that in case I found that the [enemy] had reached us, I could push her and throw her into the valley, preferring to see her dead rather than to see her captive. . . ."
> I thanked my mother for her deed, and so did my sister, who prayed that mother be rewarded [by God] in her behalf. Such solicitude [care] for honor is indeed stronger than the solicitude of men.

MARRIAGE AND MOTHERHOOD

While men's primary roles were as providers and protectors, women were expected to focus on caring for the home and children. A mother would have the assistance of other female members of the household in these tasks, including servants if the family was well-off. A man who made a good living could also have as many as four wives, but Islamic law required him to provide equal housing, clothing, food, and so on for them. He was also expected to divide his time and attention evenly among them.

Only a small minority of men had more than one wife. Women in these marriages had different experiences depending on the personalities involved. Sometimes there was bitter competition between the women. In other cases, the women became close friends, glad to have one another's help in the work of housekeeping and child rearing. Much depended on how well the husband honored his obligation to treat each wife equally. Even in the best situations, though, most women strongly preferred to be the only wife. Some even made this a condition of their marriage contracts.

WOMEN'S WORDS

Among the Bedouins of Arabia, women often played an important and admired role as poets, with the duty of praising their tribe and mourning its dead. The most famous Bedouin women poets were al-Khansa and Laila Akhyaliyya, who both lived in the mid to late seventh century. Al-Khansa is known for her poems lamenting her brother's death; we read some of her verses in chapter 3. Laila's best-known works mourned the poet and outlaw Tawba, with whom she fell in love as a young woman. Other poems of hers that have survived boast about her tribe's successes in battle and describe the animals and landscapes of her world. Here is one of them:

My camel kneels at Ibn Marwan's door
and groans three times in birth pangs.
Men circle her each night
with torches lighting the hills.
A leader and a youth bring
    companion armor
and words bright as Yemen cloth.

But crude milking injured her.
Now softly, on the slopes of Thadaq,
she's given dry food.
Then quickly to water, on good hoofs,
fast, her body lean.
Her summer offspring is unweaned
but day already smells of autumn.

Above: White camels were (and still are) rare and extremely valuable.

Nearly all women expected to marry. As in many ancient and medieval cultures, the law required that every woman have a male guardian—father, husband, or some other family member. A woman without male protection was likely to have a very difficult time; with few respectable ways to make a living, she almost certainly faced a life of poverty. This, in fact, was one reason for permitting a man to have more than one wife: it allowed him to take women under his protection who might otherwise have no one to provide for them.

When a woman married, the husband gave her a dowry. This could be money or property; often it took the form of jewelry. The dowry was the woman's to keep, to help support her in the event of divorce or widowhood. Both men and women could obtain divorces, although it was much easier for men to do so. A divorced woman typically returned to her father's family until she married again. If her children were young, they went with her, but after a certain age they were supposed to live in their father's household.

In well-to-do families, especially in cities, women and children lived a secluded life, never seeing men from outside the family. The part of the home that was kept private, off-limits to male visitors, was the harem. Depending on the size of the house, the harem might be one room or a suite of rooms. In many parts of the countryside, though, seclusion of women was not strictly practiced—for one thing, there was too much work to do, and women's help was needed with the flocks and in the fields. When women did have to leave the home to work—or to visit their women friends or go to the public bathhouse—they dressed very modestly, usually covering their hair and sometimes their faces as well. These coverings helped protect them from unwanted attention and showed that they were respectable women.

A wife attained an even higher level of respect when she became a mother, especially of a son. As a mark of that respect, she received a new name, for the rest of her life being referred to as her eldest son's mother. So if that son's name was, for example, Ali, she would be called Umm Ali, "Mother of Ali." (Similarly, Ali's father would become known as Abu Ali, "Father of Ali.") And when Ali (along with any siblings he had) was grown up, Umm Ali would likely have a place of honor in the community. As a mother of adult sons, she could exercise great influence over not only the women of the family but many of the men as well—for instance, she often played a leading role in arranging her sons' marriages.

French artist Eugène Delacroix visited North Africa in 1834 and made this watercolor sketch of women in their home.

FEEDING AND CLOTHING THE FAMILY

Women spent much of their time in food preparation. In the medieval Muslim world, even the humblest peasants were able to enjoy a healthy diet of grains, fruits, vegetables, dairy products, and meat. (In much of Christian Europe at the same period, few fruits and vegetables were eaten, and for most people meat was a rare luxury.)

Women made bread from wheat or barley flour. In places where rice was grown, they also cooked this grain to go with most meals. Many of the other ingredients village women used in their cooking were grown in their own home gardens or courtyards. Women

Rural Women

Encamped at an oasis, a woman divides her attention between her children and the fancy cap she is embroidering, while other women and a young man look after the cattle.

could raise vegetables and herbs and a few fruit trees even on a fairly small plot of ground. They might also keep a milk cow or goat and some chickens in the courtyard. Women not only had to prepare each day's meals, but they also had to preserve food to store for the coming months, since fresh produce was available only at certain seasons. Vegetables could be stored in vinegar or oil, and many fruits were made into syrups. Juices and oils were extracted from various herbs, flowers, nuts, and seeds. Grapes were dried—perhaps spread out on the flat roof of the house—to make raisins; dates and other fruits might also be dried, as were herbs. Rose petals were gathered for making rosewater, a flavorful ingredient for many dishes. Milk was turned into butter, cheese, and yogurt.

The Calendar of Córdoba mentioned many of these activities, but usually did not specify who did them, so sometimes we must make educated guesses about women's work. But certain agricul-

The Countryside

tural tasks clearly seem to have been women's specialty. For example, the Calendar of Córdoba says that in February "the women begin to tend the silkworm eggs, and wait for them to burst." Many of the other steps in the production of silk were probably also done by women, as they were later when silk working spread to medieval Italy. Women's smaller fingers (compared to men's) were felt to be better suited to handling the delicate fibers. Indeed, making thread, cloth, and clothing was one of women's main activities throughout the ancient and medieval worlds.

In the Dar al-Islam, women had a variety of materials to work with: silk, linen, cotton, wool, goat hair, and camel hair. Since silk was a luxury fiber, the average woman did not use it to make clothes for her family, but she may have been able to earn money by producing silk thread for a landowner or merchant or middleman. In the early eleventh century, the Chinese developed a belt-driven wheel to be used for unwinding the fibers from silk cocoons and winding them into thread. This invention soon found its way to India and Persia, and from there to the rest of the Middle East. Eventually it developed into a wheel for spinning wool and other fibers, and this spinning wheel finally came into use in Christian Europe in the thirteenth or fourteenth century.

Even after the arrival of the spinning wheel, though, most women during this period continued to spin in the ancient fashion, using a toplike drop spindle to twist the fibers together. Once they had enough thread spun, they could weave it into cloth. Several different types of loom were used. One of the simplest was a ground loom, which at each end had a wooden beam staked to the ground. Long threads, called the warp, were stretched between the beams. Then the woman threaded the weft yarn crosswise through the warp, weaving over and under the long threads, back and forth,

until she had the piece of cloth she needed for whatever garment or household article she was making.

A more complicated type of loom, which used foot pedals to raise and lower the warp threads (making it easier to weave the weft through them) also developed during the Middle Ages. Its use spread from al-Andalus into the rest of Europe, where it helped make possible the growth of a large-scale cloth industry. In the Islamic world, too, it was employed in many urban weaving work-shops. But the ground loom, easy to set up in a courtyard or nomad encampment, remained a more practical tool for rural women, especially Bedouin women, for many centuries to come.

Bedouin women did a huge amount of weaving—they even wove their own homes. They crafted long strips of tightly woven cloth from dark wool or goat hair or camel hair, then sewed the strips together to make tent walls and roofs. They wove many of the tent furnishings, too: rugs, cushion covers, blankets, storage bags, curtains to divide the tent into sections, and more. Both Bedouin and village women could weave either in solid colors or colorful patterns. (To make the different colors, they usually had to dye the thread themselves.) They also added color and interest to their cloth with embroidery or by sewing on narrow-woven braid. And Egyptian women during this period came up with yet another way to use thread or yarn: they created knitting, producing elaborately patterned socks, pouches, and other small, practical items.

Boys and young men were often hired to look after sheep and goats—the Prophet himself worked as a shepherd to help out his family when he was young.

FIVE

Growing Up in the Country

[The child] is a trust (placed by God) in the hands of his parents, and his innocent
heart is a precious element. . . .

↣ AL-GHAZALI, ELEVENTH-CENTURY PERSIAN SCHOLAR AND MYSTIC

CHILDREN WERE OF VAST IMPORTANCE TO MOST
people in the medieval Muslim world. Parents particularly
desired sons because they would inherit the bulk of the
family property. And since descent was traced through the male
line, sons ensured the survival of the family and tribe into the
future. Moreover, it was usually the oldest son who cared for his
parents when they became too old or ill to work.

As we have seen, parents were commonly known by the name of
their eldest son. In a family without any son, however, they could be
called Umm or Abu followed by the eldest daughter's name.
Sometimes a man who had only daughters was referred to, rather
pityingly, as Abu Banat, "Father of Daughters." But he could always

reclaim his dignity by reminding people that the Prophet, too, had been a father of daughters, since none of his sons lived past infancy. Both the Qur'an and the traditional sayings of Muhammad were very clear that daughters were as much a gift from God as sons were.

NEWBORNS AND NAMES

In the medieval Muslim world, as in most places before modern times, nearly all babies were born at home. The mother was assisted during birth by a midwife and women relatives and friends. If there were serious medical problems, a male physician might also be called in, but this was often not possible in rural areas, where few doctors worked. And although Muslim doctors and midwives had access to some of the most advanced medical knowledge and techniques of the time, these were often not enough, and many mothers and babies died during or soon after birth.

North African women and children make their way to a gathering.

Even if all went well, families waited for seven days to assure themselves that the newborn was strong enough to survive. Then they held a celebration, inviting as many guests as they could afford to feed—it was traditional to feast on a sheep or goat. Everyone gave thanks to God, and the father publicly announced the child's name.

Muslim parents often chose to name their children after important people from early Islamic history, such as Khadija and Aisha (Muhammad's wives), Fatima (Muhammad's daughter), Ali (Muhammad's son-in-law), and Husayn (Muhammad's grandson). The Qur'an was another major source for namesakes, who were also biblical figures, among them Musa (Moses), Ibrahim (Abraham), Ishaq (Isaac), Yusuf (Joseph), Sulayman (Solomon), Ayyub (Job), Yahya (John), Isa (Jesus), and Maryam (Mary). Names that contained the Arabic root meaning *praise* were very popular, too (Muhammad was one of these, as were Ahmad and Hamid), and so were names beginning with the word meaning *servant*—for example, Abd Allah (Servant of God), Abd al-Jabbar (Servant of the Almighty), and Abd al-Rahim (Servant of the Merciful).

Whatever names children were given, many people in the community would simply refer to them as the offspring of their father—so Ali's son and daughter would be called Ibn Ali and Bint Ali (Son of Ali and Daughter of Ali). *Ibn* might also be used to indicate a boy's clan membership. This was the case with, for example, the fourteenth-century historian Ibn Khaldun: Khaldun was not the name of the historian's father, but of the ancestor of their clan.

CHILDHOOD

Children were breast-fed for at least two years, which was regarded as every child's natural and legal right. Normally they were nursed by their own mothers, but if the mother had died or was unable to breast-feed because of illness or some other reason, a wet nurse would be found. The other alternative was to give the child sheep's or goat's milk; a baby bottle could be made out of animal skin or horn.

Young children stayed close to their mothers most of the time. As they grew, their parents taught them the basics of Islam and the values of the community. For both girls and boys, these values included respect for elders, loyalty to the family, honesty, modesty, compassion for the poor, patience, and trust in God. They also

A Lullaby's Comfort

All over the world, throughout human history, fussy babies have been soothed by lullabies. The Egyptian mystic Ibn al-Farid (1181—1235) included these homey images of babyhood in a poem comparing the infant's yearning for comfort to the soul's yearning for God:

When the infant moans
from the tight swaddling wrap,
and restlessly yearns
for relief from distress,

The sweet speech makes him
forget his bitter state
and remember a secret whisper
of ancient ages.

He is soothed by lullabies, and lays aside
the burden that covered him—
he listens silently
to one who soothes him.

Above: For the mystic, all aspects of nature, like the rabbit and flowers depicted on this medieval Persian tile, reflect the oneness of God.

learned the importance of hard work, without which no peasant or nomad family could survive.

Children probably started helping out almost as soon as they could toddle around. They could do such tasks as sorting lentils or beans, scaring birds away from fruit trees, pulling weeds, picking vegetables and herbs, and scattering feed for chickens. As they got stronger and surer, they could carry water from the well or other water source, bring in firewood, and so on. Girls started learning very early to spin, weave, sew, and cook. Young boys might help with some of the household work, too, for example by sorting and cleaning wool. Even with chores, though, children still had time to play. They might not have a lot of toys, but they could make playthings out of many of the objects around them, and there were no doubt a variety of games involving pretending or running or hiding and so on.

At the age of seven, children were considered able to know the difference between right and wrong. They still were not fully responsible for their actions, but they were capable of more serious learning. In some families, children might now be taught reading, writing, basic mathematics, and religious subjects, usually learning at home from their relatives or from a teacher at the local mosque; well-to-do children might have tutors. But the majority of rural children probably received little, if any, formal education. Most of them could learn everything they would need to know for their adult lives simply by following the example of their parents.

PREPARING FOR ADULTHOOD

An older boy's chores could include dealing with pests and vermin, even dangerous animals. Usama ibn Munqidh remembered that once when he was young, he and his father were standing in the courtyard of their house,

Growing Up in the Country

when a big serpent stuck its head out on the frieze of the arches of the portico over the court. My father stood in his place watching it as I carried a ladder which was on one side of the court and put it in a position below the serpent. Climbing to the serpent, under the very eyes of my father, who was watching me but not fobidding me, I pulled out a little knife from my belt, applied it to the neck of the serpent, while it was sleeping, with less than a cubit between my face and itself, and began to saw the neck. The serpent pulled its body out and wound itself around my lower arm, where it remained until I cut its head off and threw its body down to the floor of the house lifeless.

On another occasion, Usama went out with the men of the family to deal with a lion that had taken up residence at an important river crossing. When Usama faced the lion, his father, afraid for the boy's safety, yelled, "Face it not, thou crazy one! It will get thee!" Usama got the lion instead, though, and afterward remembered, "I never saw my father forbid me a fight except on that day."

Usama was probably at least a teenager by this time. Like other boys this age, he would have been considered a nearly adult man, but nowhere near ready to establish his own household yet. During the teenage years and into their twenties, males continued to learn the skills they would need to support a family, and then worked to save up enough to get married. Because they were obligated to fully provide for every member of their household, men often had to put off marriage for many years.

A girl, on the other hand, typically married around the time of puberty or soon afterward. The marriage was arranged by the bride's and groom's families, but the couple had the legal right to refuse a dis-

الله! إلى... العلم يكون رشد عند فر جنبه ده بهلوان دليره

A man trains a new horse, perhaps in preparation for riding it in a wedding or circumcision procession.

agreeable match—although girls sometimes were unable to exercise this right, either because they did not know about it or because their families pressured them to accept a particular man. Most parents, of course, took their daughter's future happiness into account and tried to choose her a husband who would treat her with love, kindness, and respect. If at all possible, they would have her marry one of her paternal cousins. This way, even though she left home to join her husband's family, she would still be part of her own extended family.

Marriage was a joyous event, and there were a variety of traditions to celebrate it; some of these are still practiced in places today. For example, before the wedding there might be a women's party during which the bride's hands and feet would be decorated with henna. The wedding itself would be an occasion for music, dancing, feasting, and fun for the whole community. Similar festivities marked a boy's circumcision, which occurred at or before puberty. This rite of purification was not prescribed by the Qur'an, but it had been traditional in Arabia since long before the coming of Islam and was considered a necessary step on the way to adulthood throughout the Islamic world.

Growing Up in the Country

Egyptian men enjoy fresh fruit and lively conversation at their midday meal.

SIX

Rest and Relaxation

There's no stronger joy for thee
Than the faces of your friends and dear ones
You can see.

↠ Rudaki, tenth-century Persian poet and musician

AMILY AND COMMUNITY CELEBRATIONS BROUGHT country people a welcome break from routine. On ordinary working days, too, people found many opportunities to socialize, even if there was less time to relax. As in any small town today, gossip was a favorite diversion. Men could chat as they walked out to the fields together or watched over the livestock. Women caught up on the latest news while they waited their turn to draw water at the village well or gathered to wash clothes in the nearest irrigation canal.

At least once a week villagers went to the local public bathhouse. Generally men and women used the same bathhouse, but on different days. A community that was home to people of different religions

often had separate bathhouses for Muslims and non-Muslims. In a small village with only one bathhouse, designated days or times might be set aside for each group. In al-Andalus, however, it was common for Muslims, Jews, and Christians to bathe together, segregated only by sex. But male or female, Muslim or non-Muslim, almost everyone looked forward to a visit to the bathhouse, which was more than a chance to get clean. Soaking in the hot water, a person could relax and daydream, or relax and chat with friends, and in general simply enjoy not working for a little while.

A marketplace in Old Cairo in the nineteenth century. Many Middle Eastern markets date back to the medieval period.

Another break from routine could be found in going to a market or fair. Here you might hear people reciting poems and telling stories, or you might sit and listen to a scholar lecture on scientific topics, including agriculture and irrigation techniques. There might be jugglers, puppet shows, and other entertainments. There might be travelers bringing news of far-off places. Above all, of course, there would be the opportunity to sell produce and livestock and to buy or trade for the useful items and foods that you couldn't make or grow yourself. You might even be able to afford a few little luxuries—

Rest and Relaxation

a bit of perfume, a piece of jewelry, or perhaps some imported spices for a special meal.

FOOD AND HOSPITALITY

One of the commonest and most enjoyable recreations was sharing a meal with family and friends. The Persian poet Ubayd-i Zakani described the pleasure he took in entertaining visitors to his country home this way:

> In my house there was always some plain bread, some greens,
>   for any guest who chanced to call
> and sometimes even a cup of wine prepared
>   for a drinking friend or a pretty girl.

Unlike the poet, most Muslims did not offer wine to their visitors, since drinking it was forbidden by the Qur'an. But they would offer the best of whatever they had, and plenty of it, even if the guests were unexpected. Hospitality and generosity were regarded as great virtues, and few things could damage a family's reputation as much as being unwelcoming or miserly.

Whether in a village house or a Bedouin tent, if it was large enough there would be a front room where guests could be welcomed. When the guests were men from outside the family, the women of the household withdrew behind a curtain or screen or stayed in another part of the dwelling. Another good place to entertain guests was the courtyard of a house. Family meals, too, were often held here. The courtyard was also where women typically did much of the cooking, working over a fire or a brazier full of hot coals. Many houses, however, did not have ovens, so women would make their bread dough at home and then take it to a public oven to bake.

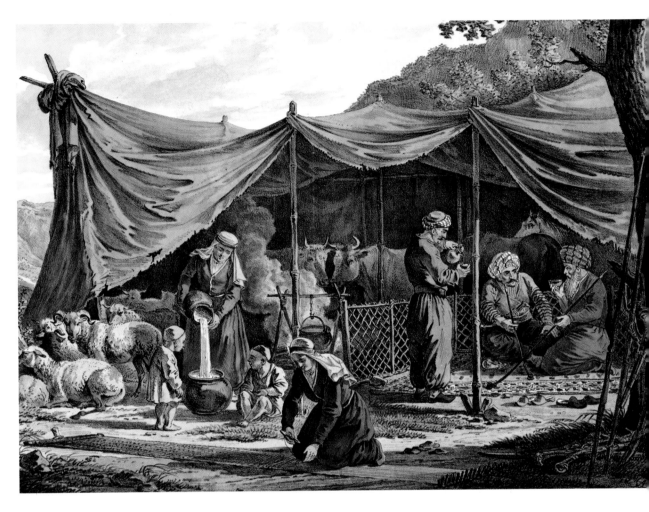

Whether a meal was family-only or included guests, it was generally served in the same way: the food was presented on a large tray set down on the floor or a very low table, and people sat on the floor around it. A guest, however, might be honored by being seated higher, on a cushion or stool or small stack of rugs. Everyone helped themselves from the tray, using mostly their fingers. (It was good manners to use only the right hand; the left was considered unclean, even though Muslim law required people to wash both hands before eating.) Food that could not easily be picked up could be scooped up with bread, and spoons were used

A Bedouin family in Lebanon in the early 1900s. A woman weaves cloth on a ground loom in front of the tent, while children watch another woman cooking, and the men talk together.

Rest and Relaxation

FESTIVE FOOD

The following recipe is for chicken *baaridah*, a Persian-style cold dish meant to be served early in a meal, before the hot food. It is based on a *baaridah* that was a favorite of a powerful government official in Baghdad, but a well-provisioned country cook could have easily prepared the same sort of thing, using herbs and vegetables fresh from the garden. The addition of pepper and cinnamon, which were luxury imports in many areas, would have made this a good special-occasion dish.

Ingredients

1 package of precooked chicken-breast strips

1/4 cup lemon juice

2 tablespoons olive oil

1 teaspoon finely chopped fresh mint

2 teaspoons finely chopped fresh tarragon

1 teaspoon finely chopped fresh thyme

1 teaspoon coriander

1/2 teaspoon pepper

1/4 teaspoon cumin

1/8 teaspoon cinnamon

1 cucumber

Instructions

Cut the chicken strips into small pieces.

Mix the lemon juice, olive oil, herbs, and spices together in a bowl.

Add the chicken to the lemon juice mixture and stir everything together.

Peel the cucumber and cut it into small pieces (about 1/4 inch).

Put the cucumber on two salad plates and mound the chicken mixture on top.

Enjoy!

Above: Many herbs and other common foods also had medical uses. This man is processing honey to use as an ingredient in medicine.

for eating soup. The meal typically began with a dish of dates and often ended with some kind of fruit salad. Neither coffee nor tea were known in the Middle East or Europe during this period, but there were many kinds of drinks made from water and juice, which came from dates, apples, oranges, lemons, grapes, pomegranates, and other fruits.

OUTDOOR ENJOYMENTS

In addition to regularly dining outdoors in the courtyard, many people liked going to picturesque spots and having picnics now and then. As they enjoyed their surroundings and one another's company, they amused themselves with conversation, stories, music, or with simply listening to the birds and smelling the flowers. On a picnic, a visit, a walk, or at home, poetry contests were another popular diversion, at all levels of society. Sometimes each person in the group had to make up a verse on the spot; sometimes one person would start a poem and challenge another to complete it. The resulting poems could be funny or dramatic, depending on the participants' moods.

Country people, especially men, spent the majority of their waking hours outdoors. They not only worked outside, but also found most of their recreation there. Men might participate in a variety of outdoor games and sports, including ball games, wrestling, and archery. Polo was popular among the wealthy, who enjoyed horse races and displays of horsemanship as well. Nomads sometimes raced camels, too.

Hunting played an important role in the countryside. It was one way that people provided themselves with meat. For many, hunting was also a form of recreation, an enjoyable sport that let a man spend the day outdoors with his friends and also put food on the table. Wealthy people had lands set aside where only they

could hunt—Usama's family, for example, "had two hunting fields, one for partridges and hares, in the mountain to the south of town; and another for waterfowl, francolins [a type of partridge], hares and gazelles, on the bank of the river in the cane fields to the west of town."

Usama's father was an enthusiastic hunter. Like other well-to-do sportsmen, he had many animals to help him on the hunt. Trained falcons and hawks brought down birds and small game such as quail and rabbit; hounds assisted in the hunting of larger quarry. To catch the largest, fastest animals—antelope, deer, and so on—wealthy hunters sometimes used trained cheetahs. A man's hunting animals were valuable and treated with great care. Usama's father, for example, had a favorite cheetah who lived in their home:

He had a special maid who served it. In one side of the courtyard she had a velvet quilt folded, with dry grass beneath. In the wall was an iron staple. After the hunt, the cheetah trainer would bring it to the door of the house in which its couching place lay, and leave it there. It would then enter the house and go to that place where its bed was spread and sleep. The maid would come and tie it to the staple fastened to the wall.

SEVEN

A Hard Life

In the garden of my life sorrow is gardener,
no tree or bush is left, no rose, no tulip.
On the threshing-floor of time, from so much pain
no ear or grain is left, no straw, no dust.

➢ KHAQANI, TWELFTH-CENTURY PERSIAN POET

OST PEOPLE IN THE COUNTRYSIDE HAD TO work extremely hard to make a living. In some ways hard work was no hardship—it was simply what was expected. Nevertheless, it could take its toll over time. For example, many kinds of farm and household work involved repetitive motions that could lead to the development of arthritis. And if a person's health or strength failed, for whatever reason, it might be difficult or impossible to keep working. This was one reason that people relied so much on their families—other than religious charity, there were no social welfare systems; only your family could be truly depended on to support you through hard times.

Opposite: The men of a North African village try to stop locusts from destroying their crops.

ENVIRONMENTAL CHALLENGES

Unfortunately, hardship could strike an entire family or community, especially if the crops failed. But total disaster could frequently be prevented, thanks to the general prosperity and wide trading networks of the medieval Muslim world. If one area lost its harvest, the people might be able to purchase food from a region that had an extra-bountiful year. Rulers, who often stored surplus grain to feed their troops and retainers, might open government warehouses and distribute grain and other staples to civilians in hard times. If these kinds of relief were unavailable, though, the results could be tragic. Such was the case when a famine struck al-Andalus in 915, causing one writer of the time to lament, "The misery of the people reached unheard-of extremes and disease and plague took such hold upon the needy that it became impossible to bury all the dead."

Crops could fail for a variety of reasons. In Egypt, for example, the Nile floodwaters were sometimes too low to fully irrigate the land; occasionally they were too high, destroying fields and homes past repair. In other places, too little or too much rainfall could be equally damaging. This was not just a problem for farmers—nomads suffered when there was not enough rain for the rough grasses their herds depended on. And even in the desert there were occasional downpours strong enough to cause flash floods, which might drown animals and people alike.

The weather was not the only natural force that country people had to contend with. Birds, insects, and wild animals could cause problems, too. Birds liked to eat ripening fruit; deer and other creatures might eat or trample vegetables and grains. Rodents got into stored food (one reason that many Muslims welcomed cats into their homes). Lions and wolves could make off with livestock. Occasionally a wild animal attacked a person—Egyptian farmers, for example, always

An Earthquake's Aftermath

Usama ibn Munqidh's story tells of the mingling of personal hardship with the tragedy of a natural disaster. As a young man, Usama quarreled with his uncle, who was governor of the Syrian province where they lived, so his uncle banished him. During Usama's exile, an earthquake struck the area. Usama's entire family was gathered in the governor's castle at the time, celebrating a circumcision, and nearly all were killed. Usama later paid a sorrowful visit to the scene:

A Persian rose, drawn by an American artist in the 1820s

All the villages have been levelled to the ground; all the inhabitants perished; the dwelling has become but a trace, and joys have been transformed into sorrows and misfortunes. I stopped there after the earthquake which destroyed it . . . and I did not find my house, nor the house of my father and brothers, nor the houses of my uncles and my uncles' sons, nor of my clan. Sorely troubled I called upon Allah in this great trial which he had sent me. . . . Then I departed . . . trembling as I went and staggering as though weighed down by a heavy load. So great was the loss that swiftly flowing tears dried up, and sighs followed each other and straightened the curvature of the ribs. The malice of time did not stop at the destruction of the houses and the annihilation of the inhabitants, but they all perished in the twinkling of an eye and even quicker, and then calamity followed upon calamity from that time onwards. And I sought consolation in composing this book and made it into a lament for the home and the beloved ones. This will be of no avail and will bring no comfort, but it is the utmost I can do. And to Allah—the glorious and great—I complain of my solitude, bereft of my family and brothers, I complain of my wanderings in alien [foreign] lands, bereft of country and birthplace.

had to be wary of the crocodiles and hippopotamuses of the Nile.

Scorpions and poisonous snakes posed a danger in many places. Some years, swarming locusts could devour an entire crop. A number of insects might carry diseases; others were simply annoying. Even annoyances could inspire poetry, though, such as these lines by an eleventh-century writer from North Africa:

Thanks for the lovely time
We spent with you last night;
The music was sublime,
The programme a delight—

The Countryside

Among the ruins of an ancient city along the Nile, villagers trap a crocodile.

The singing of the flies,
Mosquitoes on the flute,
And, as the big surprise,
The fleas that danced to suit.

WAR AND PEACE

Whatever problems country people had were always made worse by warfare. Violent and unsettled times made food shortages and epidemics more likely to occur and more severe. If enemies burned orchards or fields, it could take years for them to recover (if they ever did). Destruction of irrigation works might have even more serious

A Hard Life

consequences. After the Mongols invaded Iraq and destroyed Baghdad in 1258, there was no longer a strong enough government to maintain the countrywide irrigation system. Iraqi farmland has never been as productive as it was during the Middle Ages.

Violence could sweep down on a community as part of a full-blown war or as a lightning raid. *Razzias,* or raids, remained a part of Bedouin culture for several centuries after the coming of Islam. Raiders sometimes took not only livestock but also captives. As in the

In this illustration from a thirteenth-century Iraqi manuscript, captives are being sold in a slave market.

ancient world and much of the rest of the medieval world, people captured during any kind of warfare usually became slaves. Although slaves held by Muslims generally had more rights and more likelihood of being granted freedom than slaves would later have in the American South, many people feared capture more than they feared death. (See, for example, the story of Usama ibn Munqidh's sister at the beginning of chapter 4.)

Warfare could cause trouble for country people even when they were not directly involved in the fighting, as when armies trampled the crops. In his description of a battle in northern Syria during the Crusades, Usama ibn Munqidh noted that "the pillagers and the Arabs were scattered all over the planted fields." Crops and flocks were vulnerable whenever there were enemy forces in the land— sometimes even if peace had been declared. Usama related this episode that occurred in 1140:

> I once brought a case . . . relative to certain flocks of sheep which the [Crusader] lord of Bâniyâs had taken from the forest in the course of a period of truce between them [the Crusaders] and us. At that time, I was in Damascus. So I said to King Fulk [Christian ruler of the Crusader kingdom] . . . , "This man has trespassed upon our rights and taken away our flocks at the lambing time. The sheep gave birth and the lambkins died. Then he returned the sheep, after having lost so many of them." The king said to six, seven knights, "Arise and judge this case for him."

The knights decided unanimously that the lord of Bâniyâs should pay a hefty fine to Usama's people to make up for the damage to the flock, and King Fulk made sure that he did so.

A Hard Life

Usama told of many other incidents in which Christians and Muslims solved their differences without violence and cooperated during peacetime. Indeed, the history of the medieval Muslim world is full of instances of people of different faiths coexisting in tolerance and even friendship, working together to strengthen their communities. Remembering such achievements can give inspiration to modern people seeking to understand one another in a diverse world. We can also look back on this history in appreciation for the many benefits Muslim civilization gave to the West.

The farming practices, especially the irrigation techniques, introduced by the Muslims made an especially large impact in al-

The Countryside

Andalus and Sicily. Farmers in both places were able to bring so much more land under cultivation so efficiently that it became possible to produce as many as four harvests a year (before there had only been one, or at most two). Even after Sicily and al-Andalus came under Christian rule, Muslim farming techniques continued to be used, and these lands remained among Europe's most prosperous as a result.

And thanks to Muslim farmers and merchants, a variety of new crops found their way into Europe (and therefore, centuries later, into the Americas). Muslim traders and growers spread many beloved flowering plants, too, including lilacs, tulips, jasmine, hyacinths, and new varieties of roses. So whenever we eat rice or sugar, drink orange juice, pull on a cotton T-shirt, or admire a vase full of tulips, we are enjoying some of the great legacies of the medieval Muslim countryside.

Dates are among the many fruits that we now enjoy thanks to the farmers and traders of the Muslim world.

Glossary

al-Andalus the part of the Iberian Peninsula (modern Spain and Portugal) ruled by Muslims

Bedouin nomadic tribes of Arabia and neighboring regions

Crusade a war undertaken with the endorsement of the medieval church to bring Jerusalem and other parts of the Middle East under Christian rule. Crusaders in the eleventh and twelfth centuries established several short-lived kingdoms in what are now Syria, Lebanon, Israel, and Palestine.

mosque (Arabic *masjid*) a Muslim house of worship

paternal having to do with fatherhood or with the father's side of the family

Persia modern-day Iran

Syria during the medieval period often used as the common name for the eastern Mediterranean region, including the modern countries of Jordan, Israel, Palestine, and Lebanon as well as Syria

umma the community of Muslims

vizier (Arabic *wazir*) a chief administrator appointed by the ruler and under his direct authority

For Further Reading

Barber, Nicola. *Everyday Life in the Ancient Arab and Islamic World.* North Mankato, MN: Smart Apple Media, 2006.

Colombo, Monica. *The Islamic World: From Its Origins to the 16th Century.* Translated by Pamela Swinglehurst. Austin, TX: Raintree Steck-Vaughn, 1994.

Doak, Robin. *Empire of the Islamic World*. New York: Facts on File, 2005.

Dunn, John. *The Spread of Islam*. San Diego: Lucent Books, 1996.

George, Linda S. *The Golden Age of Islam*. New York: Benchmark Books, 1998.

Nicolle, David. *Historical Atlas of the Islamic World*. New York: Checkmark Books, 2003.

Townson, Duncan. *Muslim Spain*. Minneapolis: Lerner Publications, 1979.

Online Information

Bartel, Nick. *Medieval Islamic Cultures*.
http://www.sfusd.k12.ca.us/schwww/sch618/Islam_New_Main.html

Foundation for Science Technology and Civilisation. *Muslim Heritage*.
http://www.muslimheritage.com

Hilden, Joy May. "Tents." *The World of Beduin Weaving*.
http://www.beduinweaving.com/webarchive/tent/tent01.htm

Husn, Ma'n Abul. "Woman of Distinction: Laila Al Akhialiya."
http://www.alshindagah.com/janfeb2004/woman.html

Lunde, Paul. "Science: The Islamic Legacy."
http://saudiaramcoworld.com/issue/198203/science-the.islamic.legacy.htm

Unity Productions Foundation. *Cities of Light: The Rise and Fall of Islamic Spain*.
http://www.islamicspain.tv/Arts-and-Science/The-Culture-of-Al-Andalus/index.html

Selected Bibliography

Arberry, A. J. *Moorish Poetry: A Translation of* The Pennants, *an Anthology Compiled in 1243 by the Andalusian Ibn Sa'id.* Miami, FL: Granger Books, 1953.

Burckhardt, Titus. *Moorish Culture in Spain.* Translated by Alisa Jaffa. New York: McGraw-Hill, 1972.

Esposito, John L., ed. *The Oxford History of Islam.* New York: Oxford University Press, 1999.

Fletcher, Richard. *Moorish Spain.* New York: Henry Holt, 1992.

Hourani, Albert. *A History of the Arab Peoples.* New York: Warner Books, 1992.

Idrisi, Zohar. "The Muslim Agricultural Revolution and Its Influence on Europe." Foundation for Science Technology and Civilisation, 2005. PDF, available at

http://muslimheritage.com/topics/default.cfm?ArticleID=515

Irwin, Robert, ed. *Night and Horses and the Desert: An Anthology of Classical Arabic Literature.* Woodstock, NY: The Overlook Press, 1999.

Kennedy, Hugh. *When Baghdad Ruled the Muslim World: The Rise and Fall of Islam's Greatest Dynasty.* Cambridge, MA: Da Capo Press, 2005.

Lewis, Bernard, trans. *Music of a Distant Drum: Classical Arabic, Persian, Turkish, and Hebrew Poems.* Princeton, NJ: Princeton University Press, 2001.

Lindsay, James E. *Daily Life in the Medieval Islamic World.* Westport, CT: Greenwood Press, 2005.

Lowney, Chris. *A Vanished World: Muslims, Christians, and Jews in Medieval Spain.* New York: Oxford University Press, 2005.

McNeill, William H., and Marilyn Robinson Waldman, eds. *The Islamic World* (Readings in World History, vol. 6). New York: Oxford University Press, 1973.

Menocal, María Rosa. *The Ornament of the World: How Muslims, Jews, and Christians Created a Culture of Tolerance in Medieval Spain.* Boston: Little,

Brown and Company, 2002.

O'Callaghan, Joseph F. *A History of Medieval Spain*. Ithaca, NY: Cornell University Press, 1975.

Robinson, Francis, ed. *The Cambridge Illustrated History of the Islamic World*. Cambridge: Cambridge University Press, 1996.

Ruthven, Malise, with Azim Nanji. *Historical Atlas of Islam*. Cambridge, MA: Harvard University Press, 2004.

Zaimeche, Salah. "Muslim Contribution to Agriculture." Foundation for Science Technology and Civilisation, 2002. PDF, available at http://muslimheritage.com/topics/default.cfm?ArticleID=227

Sources for Quotations

Chapter 1

p. 13 "Since agriculture": O'Callaghan, *A History of Medieval Spain*, p. 300.

p. 19 "Round-shouldered": Burckhardt, *Moorish Culture in Spain*, p. 55.

p. 23 "The doñegal variety": Fletcher, *Moorish Spain*, p. 63.

p. 25 "It is a land": Menocal, *The Ornament of the World*, p. 84.

Chapter 2

p. 27 "Have you seen": Kennedy, *When Baghdad Ruled the Muslim World*, p. 106.

p. 33 "The whole neighborhood": *Diary of a Journey Through Syria and Palestine*, available online at http://chass.colostatepueblo.edu/history/seminar/khusraw/khusraw2.htm

p. 33 "The radish": Arberry, *Moorish Poetry*, p. 64.

p. 34 "When there is fruit": Irwin, *Night and Horses and the Desert*, pp. 226–227.

p. 35 "the dwellers in tents": ibid., p. 4.

p. 35 "I answered her": Lindsay, *Daily Life in the Medieval Islamic World*, p. 47.

Chapter 3

p. 39 "I used to have": Lewis, *Music of a Distant Drum*, p. 128.

p. 44 "Amongst the events": Idrisi, "The Muslim Agricultural Revolution," p. 18.

p. 45 "In March": Burckhardt, *Moorish Culture in Spain*, p. 67.

p. 46 "Sakhr the generous": Lewis, *Music of a Distant Drum*, p. 38.

p. 46 ". . . to him we looked": Irwin, *Night and Horses and the Desert*, p. 26.

p. 48 "When men stretched": Lewis, *Music of a Distant Drum*, p. 38.

p. 48 "was greatly addicted" and "he was hit": McNeill and Waldman, *The Islamic World*, p. 197.

p. 48 "The moment I saw": ibid., p. 196.

p. 49 "The coward": ibid., p. 196.

Chapter 4

p. 51 "No one can deny": McNeill and Waldman, *The Islamic World*, p. 204.

p. 52 "O my dear son": ibid., p. 204.

p. 53 "My camel kneels": Aliki Barnstone and Willis Barnstone, *A Book of Women Poets from Antiquity to Now* (New York: Schocken Books, 1980), p. 99.

p. 57 "the women begin": Burckhardt, *Moorish Culture in Spain*, p. 56.

Chapter 5

p. 61 "[A child] is a trust": "Al-Ghazali's Views on Children's Education," online at http://muslimheritage.com/topics/default.cfm?ArticleID=221

p. 64 "When the infant moans": Irwin, *Night and Horses and the Desert*, pp. 331–332.

p. 66 "when a big serpent": McNeill and Waldman, *The Islamic World*, p. 201.

p. 66 "Face it not" and "I never saw": ibid., p. 201.

Chapter 6

p. 69 "There's no stronger": "Persian Language and Literature: Roudaki," online at http://www.iranchamber.com/literature/roudaki/roudaki.php

p. 72 "In my house": Lewis, *Music of a Distant Drum*, p. 128.

p. 74 *Baaridah* recipe adapted from Charles Perry, "Cooking with the Caliphs,"
http://saudiaramcoworld.com/issue/200604/cooking.with.the.caliphs.htm

p. 76 "had two hunting fields": Lindsay, *Daily Life in the Medieval Islamic World*, p. 200.

p. 77 "He had a special maid": ibid., p. 201.

Chapter 7

p. 79 "In the garden": Lewis, *Music of a Distant Drum*, p. 111.

p. 80 "The misery": O'Callaghan, *A History of Medieval Spain*, p. 154.

p. 81 "All the villages": Irwin, *Night and Horses and the Desert*, p. 350.

p. 82 "Thanks for the lovely": Arberry, *Moorish Poetry*, p. 174.

p. 85 "the pillagers": McNeill and Waldman, *The Islamic World*, p. 194.

p. 85 "I once brought a case": ibid., pp. 197–198.

Index

The Countryside

Nile River, 15–16, 17, **17**, 20, 43, 80,
    82–83
nomads, **26**, 35–37, **36**, 41, 46, **47**, 48, 80
norias (water-raising machines), **18**, 19

poetry, 33, 34, 35–36, 53, 64, 72, 82–83

qanats (tunnels), 17
Qur'an, 62, 63, 67, 72
Qutayba, Ibn (writer), 35
Quzman, Ibn (poet), 33

Rabi ben Zaid (bishop), 45
razzias (raids), 46, 84
rest and relaxation, **68**, 69–72, **70–71**
    food and hospitality, 72–75, **73**, **74**
    outdoor enjoyments, 75–77, **76**

Sanawbari (poet), 34
slaves, 84–85, **84**
spinning and weaving, 57–59, **58**

Tigris River, 15–16, 17, 20
towns, 31–33, **32**
trade, 20, 22

Ubayd-i Zakani (poet), 72.39
umma, 28
Usama ibn Munqidh (noble), 48–49,
    51–52, 65–66, 76–77, 81, 85–86

villages, 28–31, **29**, **31**

warfare, 48–49, **49**, 83–87, **84**, **86**, **87**
water, 15–20, **17**, **18**, 29–30, **29**, 43–44
weather, 15, 80
women, rural, **50**, 51–52, **62**
    feeding and clothing the family,
        55–59, **56**, **58**
    marriage and motherhood, 52,
        54–55, **55**
    women poets, 53

About the Author

KATHRYN HINDS grew up near Rochester, New York. She studied music and writing at Barnard College, and went on to do graduate work in comparative literature and medieval studies at the City University of New York. She has written more than thirty books for young people, including the books in the series LIFE IN ELIZABETHAN ENGLAND, LIFE IN ANCIENT EGYPT, LIFE IN THE ROMAN EMPIRE, LIFE IN THE RENAISSANCE, and LIFE IN THE MIDDLE AGES. Kathryn lives in the north Georgia mountains with her husband, their son, and an assortment of cats and dogs. In addition to writing, she is a teacher and performer of Middle Eastern dance and music, which she has been studying for twenty years. She is always learning more. Visit Kathryn online at http://www.kathrynhinds.com

About Our Consultant

DR. JOSEF W. (YOUSEF) MERI, Fellow and Special Scholar in Residence at the Royal Aal al-Bayt Institute for Islamic Thought in Amman, Jordan, has also been a visiting scholar at the American Research Centre in Egypt; the Hebrew University of Jerusalem; L'Institut Français d'Études Arabes in Damascus; the Near Eastern Studies Department at the University of California, Berkeley; and the Institute of Ismaili Studies, London. He earned his doctorate at Oxford University, specializing in medieval Islamic history and religion and in the history and culture of the Jews of the Near East. He is the author or co-author of numerous journal articles, encyclopedia entries, and books, including *The Cult of Saints Among Muslims and Jews in Medieval Syria* (Oxford: Oxford University Press, 2002), and he was general editor of *Medieval Islamic Civilization: An Encyclopedia* (New York and Oxford: Routledge, 2006).